ANALYZE THE ANCIENTS

I0799380

ANCIENT Greece

Louise Spilsbury

Gareth Stevens PUBLISHING

Please visit our website, www.garethstevens.com.

For a free color catalog of all our high-quality books, call toll free 1-800-542-2595 or fax 1-877-542-2596.

Cataloging-in-Publication Data

Names: Spilsbury, Louise.
Title: Ancient Greece / Louise Spilsbury.
Description: New York : Gareth Stevens Publishing, 2019. | Series: Analyze the ancients | Includes glossary and index.
Identifiers: LCCN ISBN 9781538225615 (pbk.) | ISBN 9781538225608 (library bound)
Subjects: LCSH: Greece--Civilization--To 146 B.C.--Juvenile literature.
Classification: LCC DF77.S646 2019 | DDC 938--dc23

First Edition

Published in 2019 by
Gareth Stevens Publishing
111 East 14th Street, Suite 349
New York, NY 10003

© 2019 Gareth Stevens Publishing

Produced for Gareth Stevens by Calcium Creative Ltd
Editors: Sarah Eason and Jennifer Sanderson
Designers: Paul Myerscough and Jessica Moon
Picture researcher: Rachel Blount

Picture credits: Cover: Shutterstock: Nick Pavlakis; Inside: Shutterstock: 12_Tribes: pp. 31, 45; Borisb17: p. 5; Josep Curto: p. 33; Dziewul: p. 4; Elgreko: p. 20; Fritz16: p. 24; Kamira: pp. 1, 8; Lapas77: p. 42; Meirion Matthias: p. 23; Mountainpix: p. 17; Mati Nitibhon: p. 27; S-F: p. 10; Samot: p. 12; Steve Scribner: p. 6; Ralf Siemieniec: p. 37; Alexander A. Trofimov: p. 9; WitR: p. 18; Zwiebackesser: p. 11; Wikimedia Commons: p. 38; 1883: excavated by French School at Athens: p. 19; Alexmarie28: p. 39; Purchased by M. Vattier de Bourville, 1851: p. 21; Daderot: p. 28; Tilemahos Efthimiadis: p. 7; Michael Greenhalgh: p. 30; Jastrow (2007)/Campana Collection; purchase, 1861: p. 13; Jastrow (2006): pp. 22, 29, 32; Jastrow (2006); Elgin Collection: p. 16; Los Angeles County Museum of Art: p. 15; Sharon Mollerus: p. 41; Chris Nas: p. 40; Marie-Lan Nguyen (2011)/Rogers Fund, 1906, MET: p. 34; Sailko: p. 35; Bibi Saint-Pol, own work, 2007-02-08: p. 43; Ian W. Scott: p. 26; Irene Soto: p. 36; Walters Art Museum/Acquired by Henry Walters, 1925: p. 14.

All rights reserved. No part of this book may be reproduced in any form without permission from the publisher, except by a reviewer.

Printed in the United States of America

CPSIA compliance information: Batch #CS18GS: For further information, contact Gareth Stevens, New York, New York at 1-800-542-2595.

CONTENTS

CHAPTER 1

The World of Ancient Greece

The Greeks developed one of the greatest **civilizations** in the ancient world. More than 2,500 years ago, they made huge advances in science, **philosophy**, politics, art, the theater, and athletics. Those advances still have an impact on our world today.

Greek Beginnings

The first ancient Greek civilizations existed around 4,000 years ago in about 1600 BC. These civilizations were a group of small but wealthy kingdoms on mainland Greece and on the island of Crete. The Minoans in Knossos, Crete, built great cities and palaces, created beautiful art, and used a form of writing. The people of Mycenae, south of Athens, were the first to speak the Greek language. These early Greek civilizations faded out because of attacks by invaders, fires, and earthquakes. For a while, the region was in turmoil. Then by 800 BC, the ancient Greeks settled into different, powerful **city-states**.

THE PALACE AT KNOSSOS

Knossos had a huge palace filled with beautiful frescoes (wall paintings). The city's population reached more than 10,000 people at its peak.

BUILDING WALLS

The walls around Mycenae palaces are made from large blocks of stone. These blocks were carried to the mountain-top city.

City-States

The ancient Greeks were not a single united nation. They were a **culture** consisting of many city-states. Each city-state had its own laws, rulers, and government. But they all shared the same language and religion. Ancient Greek city-states included Athens, Sparta, and Delphi in Greece. Some, such as Miletus and Ephesus, were in what is now Turkey. Sometimes, the city-states worked together to fight a common enemy. For example, during the fifth century BC, **Persia** had a huge **empire**, and the Persians wanted to conquer Greece, too. The ancient Greek city-states had to fight together to defeat the Persian armies. However, some of the Greek city-states also fought each other. The two most powerful city-states were Athens and Sparta. They were great rivals who constantly fought to become the dominant power.

A Great Civilization

During the fifth century BC, Athens was the most successful city-state. It was also the center of the ancient Greek civilization. The city's leader, Pericles, built up a great trading empire. He encouraged art, science, and new ways of thinking about life. He also built many grand buildings, such as those on the Acropolis, the ruins of which still survive.

The Dawn of Democracy

One of the things ancient Greece is most famous for is its system of government: democracy. Democracy is still used in many countries today. The word "democracy" comes from Greek and means "government by the people." The earliest democracy was formed in Athens about 2,500 years ago. It involved a meeting of the **free men** of the city. They met in the agora, or central marketplace, where the main government buildings stood. The men discussed and voted on what the city should do. This system of government quickly spread to a number of other important city-states.

THE ACROPOLIS

The word "acropolis" means "high city." The Acropolis in Athens was originally a fortress with high walls. People could retreat there when the city was under attack. Later, a theater, temples, and other buildings were added to overlook the city.

FRIEZE OF ALEXANDER THE GREAT

Alexander the Great controlled a large empire. It extended from Macedonia to Egypt, and from Greece to part of India.

Spreading Greek Culture

A war was fought between Athens and Sparta from 431 BC to 404 BC. Athens lost and the city-state was captured. More wars followed. A war between the city-states of Thebes and Sparta left the Greeks in a state of disorder. In 336 BC, Alexander became king of the Greek city-state of Macedonia. After that, he took control of the ancient Greek world. He was a skilled army leader and went on to conquer new lands. He also took over the mighty Persian Empire. Alexander expanded the Greek Empire across much of Europe and Asia. He became known as Alexander the Great because he ruled the world's largest empire. As he conquered new lands, he spread the Greek language, culture, and **customs** around the world.

Examining Evidence

The ancient Greeks lived a long time ago. We know about them because we can examine evidence and objects they left behind. These range from cooking pots and artwork to the ruins of buildings and temples. This evidence gives us clues about how the ancient Greeks lived.

Studying Artifacts

Archaeologists are like history detectives. They study artifacts, or objects from the past, to learn about how people lived then. Archaeologists have found ancient Greek shipwrecks and their cargoes, which tell us what the Greeks traded. Pots and bowls decorated with scenes of everyday life tell us how the ancient Greek lived. The Romans, who ruled an empire after the Greeks, liked the ancient Greeks' buildings, statues, and paintings. They liked them so much that they copied them, and many of those copies have survived.

LEARNING FROM ARTIFACTS

Ancient Greek artifacts include useful items such as this painted vase. This vase shows us that chariot racing was one of the most popular ancient Greek sports.

The Written Word

The Greeks also left behind inscriptions, which are words carved in stone. These tell us information ranging from the names of important people to records of taxes and laws. They also wrote on **scrolls** made from papyrus—a type of paper made from the papyrus plant. The ancient Greeks were the first Europeans to write with an alphabet. Their common language and writing was one of the things that bound the ancient Greeks together. However, inscriptions tell us that they pronounced the language quite differently in different places. Finding ancient Greek inscriptions in a place tells us that the ancient Greeks ruled that area. They made the inscriptions to tell the people there something important.

ANALYZE THE ANCIENTS

This stone column was found in Ephesus, in modern-day Turkey. Using your knowledge, can you answer these questions to analyze the ancient Greeks? Check your conclusions against the Answers on pages 44–45.

1. The column has words written in the Greek alphabet and language. What does this tell us about Ephesus?

2. The ancient Greeks had a shared language. How did this help them create a Greek culture?

CHAPTER 2

Gods and Beliefs

The ancient Greeks believed in many different gods and goddesses. Each one was responsible for different parts of the world or human life. Each one also had a special power.

Stories of the Gods

The ancient Greeks believed that the home of the gods and goddesses was at the top of Mount Olympus, the highest mountain in Greece. The mountaintop was often seen above a band of clouds as though it were magically floating. The ancient Greeks believed that the gods and goddesses looked and acted a little like the people on Earth. They told many stories, called **myths**, about them. The gods had adventures and arguments, fought wars, got married, had children, and were ruled over by a god named Zeus. There were also monsters, such as Medusa, whose gaze turned people to stone, and Cyclops, who had one eye in the middle of his forehead.

THE HIGHEST MOUNTAIN

Ancient Greeks believed Mount Olympus was the home of the gods. They also believed it was the site of the throne of Zeus.

KING OF THE GODS

Zeus was believed to sit on Mount Olympus. He watched and ruled the other gods and the humans on Earth.

Greek Gods

These are a few of the most important ancient Greek gods and goddesses.

- Zeus was king of the gods and the god of thunder and lightning. He could control the weather.
- Poseidon was the brother of Zeus and the god of the sea. He could make freshwater gush from Earth. When he was angry, he could cause earthquakes.
- Athena was the goddess of war and wisdom. Most Greek cities had a building dedicated to Athena, the "protector of the city." Athens was named after her.
- Hermes was the protector of travelers and the messenger of the gods. He had a stick that could make men instantly fall asleep.
- Demeter was the goddess of new life, plants, and farming. It was believed that she made the crops grow each year
- Hades was god of the dead in the **Underworld**. One of his special powers was invisibility.

Temples and Worship

The ancient Greeks believed it was important to do things that pleased their gods so that the gods would help them. If the gods were displeased or unhappy, they punished people.

Temple Worship

The ancient Greeks wanted to show the gods and goddesses how important they were to people. So they made their temples very large and grand, with stone columns along the front. The temples had beautifully carved statues of the god or goddess to whom the temple was dedicated. Priests, whom the ancient Greeks believed could talk to the gods, cared for the temples. This meant that the priests were very important and well respected. One of the most famous Greek temples is the Parthenon in the Acropolis in Athens. It was built for the goddess Athena.

APOLLO'S TEMPLE IN DELPHI

People from all over the ancient Greek world came to visit this important temple. It was built at Delphi in Greece for the god Apollo.

Rituals and Sacrifices

Some of the **rituals** carried out to worship the gods were simple. People prayed and gave **offerings** of food and flowers to ask for things such as a good harvest. Some rituals were complicated festivals held in honor of a god. These festivals included music, competitions, parades, and animal **sacrifices**. Animals such as goats and sheep were cleaned and decorated with flowers. This made them special and pure. They were taken to the temple **altar** by a parade of people and musicians wearing special robes. After the animal was sacrificed at the altar, the fat and bones were burned for the gods. The meat was cooked and eaten in a feast. Every part of the ritual had to be done the same way every time or it would not please the gods.

ANALYZE THE ANCIENTS

This vase painting shows an animal sacrifice. Can you answer these questions to analyze the ancient Greeks?

1. Why do you think the boar being sacrificed has a garland of flowers around its neck?

2. One priest is kneeling and the other is preparing to sacrifice the animal in a particular way. Why was it important to follow the rituals precisely?

The Underworld

The ancient Greeks prayed, gave offerings, and made sacrifices. They believed they had to do this to make sure their gods and goddesses would take care of them while they were alive. They also believed that their gods took care of them after they died when they went to the Underworld.

Funeral Rituals

Ancient Greeks believed that after they died, their **souls** lived on as a sort of ghost. They believed that a funeral had to involve certain specific rituals to make sure their soul went to the Underworld. Otherwise, it would stay on Earth to haunt people. First, female relatives cleaned and dressed the dead person's body. Then the body was taken to the cemetery in a funeral **procession** just before dawn. During the procession, women tore at their hair and clothing to show they were in **mourning**. At the cemetery, the body was put in a grave, sometimes along with a few objects. A rectangular **tombstone** or mound of earth was placed over the grave. Ancient Greeks often added stone columns or statues to mark the grave. This was to make sure the dead person would be remembered.

FUNERAL PROCESSIONS

This decorated plaque shows a family in mourning around the body of their relative. Some mourners pull at their hair in sadness.

HADES AND CERBERUS THE GUARD DOG

In one Greek myth, Hercules had 12 dangerous tasks to complete. One was to kidnap Cerberus. He succeeded, but later returned the three-headed dog to Hades in the Underworld.

Going to the Underworld

The ancient Greeks believed that when a body was buried, the soul traveled to the land of the dead. To get there, the soul had to cross an underground river called the Styx. The dead were buried with a coin in their mouth to pay the ferryman, Charon. He took the dead across the river. Hades had a vicious three-headed dog named Cerberus who guarded the gates to the Underworld. He stopped people from trying to escape. At the gates, three judges decided where to send each soul. People who had lived a good life went to a comfortable, sunny place called Elysium. But people who had lived a bad life went to a horrible place called Tartarus, where they received terrible punishments.

CHAPTER 3

Art and Culture

The art, culture, and ideas of the ancient Greeks had a huge impact on the world and still affect us today.

Artists and Thinkers

Ancient Greece was home to many bright and talented people. Philosophers such as Socrates, Plato, and Aristotle came up with many ideas about how the world worked. Herodotus was the first person to research and organize information about the past in a history book. Pythagoras made important discoveries in math. A math formula used to figure out the length of the sides of triangles was named after him. Greek doctors, such as Hippocrates, tried to figure out the reasons for illness and disease. Artists and sculptors found more natural and realistic ways of representing the world. They made paintings on vases and walls, and carved stone sculptures called friezes.

PARTHENON FRIEZE

This beautiful stone carving was made by talented sculptors in ancient Greece. It is from the Parthenon.

Greek Architecture

Greek **architecture** has influenced building design ever since it began. Greek buildings often used upright posts, called columns. Horizontal beams across the top of the columns could be used to form a roof.

The columns were in one of three main styles:

- Doric columns were the oldest, simplest, and thickest. They have no base and the columns have a very simple shape at the top.
- Ionic columns were thinner than Doric columns, and the tops featured scrolls and a slightly decorated base.
- Corinthian columns were the most decorative of all. They often had leaves and floral patterns at the top.

Buildings in ancient Greece all followed a set of rules. This made sure that the buildings were similar and that they were all strong and built to last. The rules told builders how wide or how high the columns should be. They also said how many columns a building should have. Above the columns on a Greek building was often a decorative panel that told a story or recorded an important event.

CORINTHIAN COLUMNS

These are the ruins of an ancient Greek temple with four Corinthian columns.

Greek Theater

The ancient Greeks were the first people in the world to go to a theater to see a play. Some of the plays written and performed in ancient Greece are still performed today. Among the most famous Greek playwrights were Sophocles, Euripides, and Aristophanes.

Greek Theaters

There was a theater in almost every Greek city. Theaters were large and often built into a hillside. They were very grand and important buildings. They were built like open-air **amphitheaters**. They were semi-circular, with rows of tiered stone seating around the open central area. Some were enormous, with seats for up to 18,000 people. The bowl-shaped design made sure everyone in the audience had a good view. The shape also brought sound upward, so the audience could hear sounds, music, and the actors' voices. At first, theater was not just a form of entertainment. It was also a way to worship their gods during religious festivals. So, in the center of the circle at the bottom, there was an altar for sacrifices.

THE THEATER IN EPIDAURUS

This ancient Greek theater is in Epidaurus, Greece, and was built in 340 BC.

DIONYSUS MASK

Greek theater masks were made of stiff, painted linen material, so none have survived. We know what they looked like because the Greeks also made clay models of them. This mask is of the god Dionysus.

Greek Plays

Greek audiences watched different types of play. These plays included tragedies, in which bad and sad things happened, and comedies, which made the audience laugh. All the actors were men or boys, even for women characters. The story was told by a large group of men called the chorus. They spoke, sang, and sometimes danced together on a flat area called the orchestra. Later, a raised area called a stage was added for solo performers. Actors wore wigs and big masks with larger-than-life features. The masks had a large mouth hole to help make their voices louder. The masks told the audience what type of character an actor was playing. For example, it showed whether he was evil or good. Some masks had two sides. The actors could turn them around to change their mood for different scenes. The best actors could also win prizes.

CHAPTER 4

Soldiers at War

The ancient Greeks were often at war. There were wars between different city-states, such as Athens and Sparta. There were also wars between the Greeks and invaders such as the Persians.

Ancient Greek Soldiers

A few rich soldiers could afford a war horse and rode into battle. However, most Greek soldiers fought on foot. They were called hoplites, named after their hoplon shield. Most hoplites had to buy their own armor. Rich men could afford metal armor to protect their chest. However, most soldiers wore cheap armor made from leather and linen glued together. Hoplites wore **bronze** shin guards to protect their legs. They wore sandals on their feet, all year round. Bronze helmets covered most of a soldier's face. Later designs were more open so soldiers could see better in battle. Helmets often had a curved part called a crest sticking above the helmet. It was designed to make a soldier look taller and fiercer.

HOPLITES IN BATTLE

This image of hoplites fighting is from an ancient Greek jug.

Spartan Soldiers

Spartan soldiers were the fiercest soldiers of all. The city-state of Sparta focused on creating the strongest army and the best soldiers in Greece. In Sparta, boys had to leave their family homes at the age of seven and go to a military school. They stayed at the school until they became soldiers at the age of 20. Training was tough and Spartan soldiers lived in harsh conditions. They were given only one tunic. They marched everywhere in bare feet, even when it was freezing cold. The soldiers were not given much food to eat and they were often beaten. They were also encouraged to fight each other to improve their fighting skills.

ANALYZE THE ANCIENTS

This is a replica of a Greek soldier's helmet. Can you use your knowledge to answer these questions about it?

1. Why are the eye openings so large?

2. Why is there a crest on top of the helmet?

Weapons of War

The weapons ancient Greeks used in battle were powerful and advanced for their time.

Ancient Greek Weapons

A hoplite's main weapon was a spear with a sharp metal point at both ends. It was 9 feet (2.7 m) long and was used for stabbing enemy soldiers. Hoplites also carried a large round shield made from wood. It was sometimes covered in a layer of bronze metal. Soldiers personalized their shields with their own designs, such as the **symbol** of their family or city. Some also carried a straight, double-edged sword with an iron blade. The soldier could swing the sword to stab and attack enemy soldiers. These swords were expensive. Since soldiers had to buy their own swords and pay to be trained to use them, not many could afford a sword.

SOLDIERS' SHIELDS

This is a model of an ancient Greek shield. Groups of hoplites used their large shields to push forward into enemy armies.

TRIREME WARSHIPS
This is a model of an ancient Greek triple-decker warship known as a trireme.

Battle Tactics

Hoplites were trained to fight in groups. They formed lines and locked their shields together, with their spears pointing over the top. This formation was called a phalanx. A team of hoplites moved forward together like this, with a wall of shields in front of them. It was very hard for enemy soldiers to break through a phalanx.

Warships

The trireme was a triple-decker warship that ruled the waves in ancient Greece. At 121 feet (37 m) long and 18 feet (5.5 m) wide, they were quite large. But they were also light so they could move quickly. They were powered by 170 oarsmen, pulling 3 rows of oars each side. There were 31 men in the top, 27 in the middle, and 27 in the bottom. Triremes were armed with a long, wooden ram tipped with bronze. This ram could split open enemy warships. Soldiers onboard could also fire spears and shoot arrows at the enemy. They could also try to board enemy ships to attack.

Famous Battles

The ancient Greeks were often at war. But some wars and battles are more famous or were more important than others.

Battle of Marathon

At the Battle of Marathon in 490 BC, an army of about 10,000 Greeks fought 20,000 Persians led by King Darius. The Greeks surprised the Persians by charging straight at them. In a single afternoon, they pushed back their enemies and prevented the Persians from invading Greece. The battle is best remembered for the amazing deed of a Greek messenger. The messenger was said to have run about 25 miles (40 km) from Marathon to Athens after the battle. He went to tell the city's leaders that the Greeks had won. He ran so fast that he collapsed and died on arrival. Marathon races people run today are named after this event.

ATHENIAN TREASURY

Greek city-states paid tributes of money to Athens for protection against the Persians. Valuables were stored in this treasury in Athens.

Sparta Versus Athens

The two city-states—Sparta and Athens—fought the Peloponnesian War, from 431 BC to 404 BC. At first, Athens was winning. The city had built long walls all the way from the city to its port. The Spartans could not break through them. Later, the Spartans managed to defeat the Athenian ships. The city could no longer get new supplies of food from the sea. When the people of Athens began to starve, they surrendered. The city of Athens was then captured.

TROJAN HORSE

This statue of the great mythical Trojan horse is from Turkey. It is the site of ancient Troy.

The Trojan Horse

A story from one of the most famous Greek battles probably never happened. Instead, it was a Greek legend. This legend tells the story of how the Greeks conquered the city of Troy (in modern-day Turkey) in 1180 BC. Soldiers hid inside a giant wooden horse, which they left outside the city's walls. The people of Troy thought it was a gift, so they wheeled it inside the city walls and shut the gates. During the night, the soldiers who had been hiding inside attacked and defeated the city. Historians believe there was a Trojan war, but no wooden horse.

CHAPTER 5

Work and Trade

There were many jobs for men in ancient Greece. As well as becoming soldiers or farmers, men could be sailors, fishermen, teachers, government workers, potters, builders, metalworkers, or stone-carvers.

Farmers

Many ancient Greeks were farmers. Greece has hot, dry summers with most rain falling in winter. Only about one-fifth of the land was good for growing crops, so farming was hard work. The main crops were grapes for wine, olives for oil, and grains such as wheat, millet, and barley. Farmers also grew broad beans, chickpeas, and lentils. Farm tools were quite basic. Farmers mostly did digging, weeding, plowing, and harvesting by hand. They used wooden or iron-edged plows, hoes, and sickles. Some wealthy farmers had oxen to help them pull the plows.

BILLY GOAT

This is an ancient Greek statue of a goat. Goats were commonly raised by farmers to provide meat, wool, and milk.

Other Jobs

People in ancient Greece had a wide variety of jobs. Some men made crafts that could be **exported** and exchanged for items that their own city-state lacked or wanted. Bards wrote poetry and performed it in public readings. Cart drivers carried heavy loads of crops, goods, or building materials. Messengers delivered messages between people and cities. Magistrates enforced laws. Masons built brick and stone buildings. Mathematicians calculated with numbers. Musicians were paid to play instruments, such as the flute and lyre. They played at public events, and some wealthy families also paid them for private performances. Some rich Greek men owned and managed large estates. A slaver was a man who followed armies fighting in battle. He captured the people they defeated. He then sold them to rich Greeks as **slaves**. Slaves were forced to work for nothing more than a daily meal and were mainly used to work on farms. Even small landowners might own one or two slaves.

ENTERTAINING THE RICH

Musicians entertained rich Greeks at feasts and festivals.

Arts and Crafts

There were skilled craftspeople in ancient Greece who made different types of arts and crafts. The ancient Greeks decorated buildings, streets, and the inside of their homes. They wanted beautiful objects wherever they went.

Metal and Stone Workers

Some craftspeople made metal weapons. Others made bowls and vases, cooking pots, drinking cups, and lamps. Tools and weapons were often made of tough iron or bronze. Bronze was also used to make statues. Sculptors created beautiful sculptures of gods, war scenes, and myths for religious worship and decoration. Metal workers made jewelry such as necklaces and bracelets out of more expensive metals, such as gold and silver. Some craftspeople made mosaic pictures from many small pieces of colored glass, pottery, or tiles. Rich people also had floors decorated with mosaics.

DERVENI KRATER

This is the Derveni Krater. This beautiful container made from bronze and tin was found in a tomb. It was used to hold the remains of a rich man and his wife.

RED-AND-BLACK POTTERY

This red-and-black pottery jar shows Apollo playing a lute. The ancient Greeks believed that Apollo invented that musical instrument.

Painters and Potters

We know about Greek paintings because they are mentioned in Greek histories written at the time. People could walk down streets where the walls were colorfully painted with scenes of warriors, hunts, and myths. Those paintings faded over time and most were lost. Some paintings survived in Greek tombs. Those paintings were not exposed to the wind, heat, sunlight, rain, and other things that ruined the outside paintings.

Other craftspeople made many types of pottery in different shapes and sizes. These ranged from simple clay cooking pots to vases. Some were painted with very detailed designs and scenes from daily life. These give us a lot of important information about how the ancient Greeks lived. Greek potters developed a special technique that required three stages of firing. This technique produced the red-and-black pots for which the ancient Greeks are most famous.

Merchants and Markets

Sea surrounds the country of Greece. This made it easy for the ancient Greeks in their powerful ships to transport goods. In doing so, they traded with other countries and spread the Greek culture and way of life.

Trade in Action

The ancient Greeks built trading stations or trading posts near the sea in foreign places. They had Greek pottery, bronze, silver, and gold pots, olive oil, wine, and cloth. They traded these items for luxury items and raw materials that were hard to get in Greece. Farmers around Athens grew wheat and barley, but not enough to feed the city-state's vast population. So they also had to trade for grain from various suppliers, mainly in Egypt, the Black Sea, and Sicily.

POTTERY FOR TRADE

This ancient Greek pottery shows a young man leading his donkey. Greek pottery was traded throughout the Greek Empire.

From Exchange to Coin Change

Early trade in ancient Greece was mainly carried out by exchanging one type of item for another. This was called the barter system. Later, some goods were exchanged for bronze or copper metal bars, then smaller rods. Everyone agreed on a certain value for these bars. The next step was to make metal coins, which were easier to carry. They could be exchanged for any goods or services. The first Greek coins appeared in around 600 BC. They were silver and stamped with designs that told people which city made them and guaranteed their value. The most famous ancient coin from Athens is the tetradrachm. It has the goddess Athena, the protector of Athens, on one side. On the other side is her owl mascot, which is a symbol of wisdom and of Athens.

ANALYZE THE ANCIENTS

This is both sides of an ancient Greek coin. Can you use your knowledge to answer these questions about it?

1. Can you tell which city-state made the coin? How do you know this?

2. What does the symbol of the owl represent?

CHAPTER 6

Everyday Life

Everyday life was tough for most ancient Greeks. Most were poor because good farmland, wood for building, and water were hard to find. Life in ancient Greece varied for rich and poor. It was also quite different for men and women.

Men and Women

Ancient Greece was run by men, and only free men could vote in its democracy. Men left the family home each day to go to work. Men were in charge of the family and the home. Women were expected to stay in the house. They had to obey their father or husband, and had to ask permission even to leave the house. Female slaves might run errands in public, but most rich women were not allowed to go out, even to the market. They cared for children, cleaned, and cooked. They also spun and wove cloth. They then sewed the cloth into bedding, wall hangings, rugs, and clothes. Some women helped in their husband's business. The wife might cook, bake bread, or weave for him. This was only if the family could not afford enough slaves to do all the work.

POOR WOMEN OF ANCIENT GREECE

Poor women could go out alone to shop for food, fetch water, and wash laundry in a stream.

WOMEN OF TANAGRA

These beautifully carved figures show wealthy women of Tanagra, north of Athens, in around AD 4.

The Difference in Sparta

Life for the women of Sparta was different from those of other city-states. Sparta's girls and women were expected to go outdoors and exercise. They were expected to do things to keep fit and strong. In Sparta, women had more say in how their home and their city were run. This was partly because Spartan men were always fighting or training for war. They expected the women to run the farms and cities. They expected the women to give orders to the slaves who were owned by the city. By the fourth century BC, Spartan women owned more than one-third of all Spartan land. Some Spartan women were very wealthy and powerful.

Houses and Homes

Most ancient Greeks lived in villages or in the countryside around a city. Rich homes in the city and poor peasant houses were fairly simple. They were all built for the same purposes. One purpose was to keep men and women separate. Another was to keep people cool in summer and warm in winter.

Greek Homes

Women were not allowed to eat or sleep in the same rooms as men. Two-story houses may have had a kitchen, storage rooms, a toilet, and sometimes an animal pen on the ground floor. On the ground floor, there would also be a room where the man of the house and his friends met. The man and his guests were served food and entertained by slaves. Rooms for the women and children were usually separate and often on the second floor of the house. Women had to stay in the parts of the house farthest from the front. This was so they could not be seen from the outside. Houses usually had rooms leading off a central open **courtyard**. The courtyard let in a lot of light and let air flow through. The walls of houses were often made from wood and mud bricks. Window holes were always small. They had shutters to keep out the sun.

MOSAIC FLOORS

The floors of wealthier homes were covered in beautiful and complicated mosaics.

BATHHOUSES

These are the ruins of an ancient Greek bathhouse at Knossos.

Home Life

The courtyard often contained an altar where the family could pray, a well for water, and a space where women could weave. Workshops for the family business were often attached to the house or even inside it. Homes did not contain much furniture, especially if the owners were poor. Chairs and stools were made of wood. Beds were made from a wooden frame with a board at the head. Bands of leather hide were laced across to create the bed. Animal skins were placed on top. Wooden chests were used to store clothes. In rich people's homes, the walls and floors were decorated with colorful mosaics and paintings. Most people went to a stream or public bath to wash. Some rich families had baths at home, filled with water carried by their slaves.

Food and Fashion

For most Greeks, the food they ate and the clothes they wore were simple. Richer Greeks could afford more decorative clothes and ate a larger variety of food.

LAVISH BANQUETS

This banquet scene was painted on a tomb of a wealthy person in Thessaloniki, Greece.

Greek Food

The ancient Greeks used the grains they grew and **imported** to make different kinds of bread. For breakfast, they usually ate bread and fruit. For lunch, they ate more bread, this time with cheese. They made barley into a kind of porridge. They ate it for dinner with cheese, fish, and seafood such as octopus, vegetables, eggs, and fruit. Only wealthy people could afford to pay hunters to catch meat such as hare, deer, and wild boar. Everyone ate olives or used olive oil for cooking.

Greek Clothes

Ancient Greeks all wore tunics. A woman's long tunic, or chiton, was made from one large piece of linen or cotton. They wore a cloak over their chiton. Young men wore short tunics, and men wore long tunics. The wealthier the person, the more colorful their tunic was. Slaves wore a small strip of cloth called a loincloth wrapped around their waist. Jewelry was mostly worn by rich women and sometimes men. It was worn as a symbol of wealth and power, to celebrate the gods, and to ward off evil. Gold was very valuable and was used to make special jewelry. Wealthy people were often buried with gold items to show off their wealth and status. Wreaths made from leaves were first given as prizes in the Olympics and other competitions. Later, rich and important Greek men wore headbands of gold leaves. These were for special occasions and to signify great honors.

ANALYZE THE ANCIENTS

This is an ancient Greek headband. Can you answer these questions about it?

1. Why is this headband made in the shape of a wreath of leaves?

2. Who is most likely to have worn this headband and why?

Growing Up

Growing up in ancient Greece could be very different. It depended on whether the person was a boy or a girl, or rich or poor.

Bringing Up Babies

In ancient Greece, daughters got married and left home. The girl's family also had to give an expensive gift to her husband's family. A son stayed home and helped in the family business. He also looked after his parents when they were old. This meant that parents often preferred sons to daughters. When a baby was born, the father could decide whether to keep it. If the baby was weak or it was a girl, he might order the baby to be left outdoors to die.

WOMEN'S ROLE

In ancient Greece, women had little power. Their main role was to give birth to children.

TOYS FOR CHILDREN

Children in ancient Greece played with toys much like children do today. This little horse could be pulled along with a string.

Girls

Daughters were brought up by their mothers or female hired help. They had to learn how to run a home, so they were taught to cook, weave, and clean. They also learned songs and dances to perform at religious festivals. Some girls in rich families were taught to read and write, but that was very unusual. At the age of 15, or sometimes younger, wealthy fathers chose a man for their daughter to marry. The daughter married and had to leave the family home. The daughters of poor families were more likely to meet a husband while working in the fields.

Boys

Boys were able to go to school if their family could afford to pay the teacher's bills. They started school at six years old. Boys learned reading, writing, math, and poetry. They were also taught to play musical instruments. Being strong and fit was also important to the Greeks. Boys learned sports such as wrestling, running, jumping, and javelin throwing. In Sparta, boys and girls were taught athletics. When boys were 16, they trained for their future jobs.

The End of Ancient Greece

Alexander the Great helped spread Greek culture across the ancient world. After he died at the age of 33, there was no obvious person to take over his empire. Greek power began to weaken.

The Romans

After Alexander the Great's death in 323 BC, his generals divided the Greek empire among themselves. This was unsuccessful because they all wanted power. They began to fight against each other, and battles between them raged for 30 years. As a result, Roman armies began to take over parts of the Greek empire. By 146 BC, Greece and Macedonia had become part of the Roman Empire. In fact, the name Greece was given to the region by the Romans. The Greeks called themselves Hellenes and they called their country Hellas.

RUINS OF THE EMPIRE

These are the ruins of an ancient Greek temple in Sicily. The island of Sicily, which is below Italy, was once part of the Greek world.

ROMAN COPIES

Greek culture lived on after ancient Greek power ended, in part because the Romans made copies of ancient Greek sculptures, such as this one of Eirene and the infant Ploutos. Eirene represents peace and Ploutos represents wealth.

Greek Culture Continues

The Greek Empire had come to an end and was under Roman rule. But Greek identity was not entirely lost. The city-states continued to govern themselves, but they were watched closely by the Romans. Romans started to visit the ancient Greek cities, such as Athens and Sparta. The Romans saw the ancient Greek culture for themselves. They studied and copied many parts of Greek culture, from its art to its buildings. They even had replicas, or copies, made of Greek statues that they liked. They put the statues in Roman homes and cities. The Greek language spread, too. It was probably spoken in Rome as often as the Roman language, Latin. Greek ideas, art, and culture became a huge influence on the Romans. They also became a central feature of the Roman world. This is partly why many of the achievements of the ancient Greeks are known to us today.

Answers

Did you manage to analyze the ancients? Check your answers against the correct answers on these pages.

PAGE 9

1. The column with Greek letters tells us that Ephesus was part of the ancient Greek world long ago.
2. Their common language and writing was one of the things that bound the ancient Greeks together and helped them develop their civilization.

PAGE 13

1. The garland of flowers around the boar's neck shows that it is special and has been made pure.
2. Priests had to carry out ritual sacrifices in the same way every time so that they worked properly and so that they pleased the gods.

PAGE 21

1. The men race while wearing their armor to remind everyone that sport is important for keeping fit and strong for war.
2. Their shields are all the same size and weight to keep the race fair.

PAGE 23

1. The helmets had wide eye holes so that soldiers could see better in battle.
2. Helmets often had a curved part called a crest sticking above the helmet to make a soldier look taller and fiercer.

PAGE 33

1. The coin is from Athens because it has the goddess Athena on it, who is the protector of Athens.
2. Owls are symbols of wisdom, so they represent the goddess Athena, who is the goddess of war and wisdom. The owl is also the symbol of the city of Athens.

Answers

PAGE 39

1. Wreaths made from leaves were first given as prizes in Olympics and other competitions. They show a person's success.
2. This headband was probably worn by a rich and important Greek man for special occasions and to signify great honors. We know this because it is in the shape of a wreath and made from gold. Gold was used to make special jewelry for rich people to show off their wealth and status.

Glossary

altar a table or platform where religious rituals are carried out

amphitheaters oval or circular theaters with stepped seats around an open central space for spectators to watch contests and races

architecture the science of building

bronze a metal made from a mixture of tin and copper, which are metals found in rock

city-states cities that, with their surrounding areas, form an independent state

civilizations settled and stable communities in which people live together peacefully and use systems such as writing to communicate

courtyard an area without a roof that is surrounded by walls, usually in the center of a house

culture the beliefs, customs, and arts of a particular group of people or country

customs the traditional actions or behaviors of people in a particular group or place

empire a large area of land or group of countries ruled over by one leader

exported bought or brought from one country and sold to another

free men men who are not slaves

imported bought or brought in from another country

mourning the expression of deep sadness after someone has died

myths stories from ancient times that explain natural or social events and that usually involve supernatural beings or events

offerings things that people give as part of a religious ceremony or ritual

Persia a historical region in southwestern Asia that is now Iran

philosophy the study of ideas about knowledge, truth, and the meaning of life

procession a number of people or vehicles moving in an orderly way

rituals ceremonies performed for religious reasons

sacrifices animals or people killed to honor a god or gods

scrolls rolls of paper

slaves people who are owned by other people, and have to obey them and work for them

souls people's inner essence or spirit that some people believe lives on after their body dies

symbol an image that represents something else

temples buildings where people go to worship their god or gods

tombstone a stone placed over a grave

tributes gifts of food and other items paid by people to their ruler

Underworld the mythical world of the dead

wreath a band, hoop, or ring of flowers or leaves